BEGIN AGAIN

How to Heal From Divorce & Create a Life You Love as a Single Mom

Deidra Romero

Begin Again © Copyright 2024 Deidra Romero

For more information, email deidraromero@gmail.com.

ISBN: 979-8-9899284-0-8

DOWNLOAD THE BEGIN AGAIN WORKBOOK

To get the best experience with this book, I've found readers who download and print the Begin Again workbook (it's free!) are able to process these big ideas easier. There's something magical about writing it all out.

You can grab your copy by visiting:
www.deidraromero.com/workbook

DEDICATION

For Lisa
Who lit the path for me, so I can light it for others

.

TABLE OF CONTENTS

INTRODUCTION

"Sometimes we feel that we are barely pulling ourselves forward through a tight tunnel on badly scraped-up elbows. But we do come out the other side, exhausted and changed." —— Anne Lamott, *Stitches*

This isn't a book I wanted to write. I never wanted these credentials or the title of "single mom." I couldn't even say the word "divorce" for the first six months of my separation. The syllables wouldn't come out. "My marriage is ending." "Mark moved out." That's what I said instead.

This is not how I thought my life would go.

But as crazy as this sounds, I am grateful for it all. Learning to live a fully integrated story is part of the path ahead of you. Remembering the wonderful things about your married life—that trip to Mexico, the births of your children, that one birthday party... and holding those memories in your hands with the bad ones too—that big fight the day after Christmas, the time he said that thing that you'll never forget, the really bad depressive episode.

Throughout this book I'll quote two people over and over: my therapist, Sharon, and Anne Lamott, my matron saint who guided me through divorce recovery. I owe them both more than I can ever repay.

In her beautiful book *Stitches,* Anne writes about how we piece our lives back together after tragedy and loss stitch by stitch.

"When you watch people you love under fire or evaporating, you realize that the secret of life is patch patch patch. Thread your needle, make a knot, find one place on the other piece of torn cloth where you can make one stitch that will hold. And do it again. And again. And again."

This divorce recovery work in front of you is holy. It is the work of healing. From rags and tattered shreds, you're making one sturdy stitch at a time.

I wish you didn't need this book. But no matter what your divorce story is, I know damage has been done to you and probably those you love. Whether you are the one who was left, or you did the leaving, *this book is for you.* If you were betrayed or if you were unfaithful (in any capacity), *this book is for your grief, too.* If you lost more things than you can count, this book is definitely for you. If you still can't get out of bed some days when you don't have your kids, I promise you, we will find some hope for you in these pages.

This is the book I wish I had when I was going through my divorce recovery, especially in those very dark, early days. I had zero resources, except for my two friends who had already walked through divorce. Use this book as a roadmap. My hope is that it pushes you further toward your healing by giving you some actionable tools and shifting your mindset. In these pages I've summarized my own path to healing and wholeness.

In the last four years of my divorce recovery journey, I've met so many wonderful people who have gone through their own traumatic divorces. People heal differently and at their own pace. **But not everyone heals.** This is really important for you to know. Healing is an option. It's not a time thing. *Oh, how I wish it was that simple.* Not everyone chooses to take this huge tragedy, stand it up on its end and jump off it. But that is what you are doing, and you are so incredibly brave for showing up.

This book is intended for women who are either separated or divorced, and the decision to split from their spouse is final. I really don't think you can start to move toward healing and recovery if you are still in that limbo stage of separation. We can't rebuild your life after divorce if you aren't sure the divorce is happening. That being said, it doesn't matter if it was ten years ago or ten days ago. If you still feel you have healing work to do, this book will give you a starting point.

Before we go any further, I think it's imp[
define healing and divorce recovery. What does
Divorce recovery is the act and the process
through now. It is the road to healing. When I t[
I am not talking about the absence of pain.
less (more about this later) but don't fool yours[
the pain means you aren't healing. Healing after divorce means
you are no longer held hostage by the pain and resentment and
somehow you've found gratitude for it all. That last piece, *oof* …

In my experience, there really are five keys to help you
heal in these early stages. There are many more, but these are
the foundation to learning how to rebuild your life. I'll break
these down and give you some writing exercises to set things in
motion.

I call these keys **PRESS** to help me remember each one.

Plan – We'll talk about how to develop a plan for your life
to help you move forward.

Responsibility – We'll figure out where you need to take
responsibility for your divorce.

Empowerment – We've got to step into empowerment and
get you out of a victim mindset. This is crucial to your recovery.

Storytelling – I'll teach you how to tune into the narratives
you're telling yourself and why this is pivotal to your healing.

Support – Connection is essential to your healing journey.
I'll explain how you can find and tap into your support system.

I've intentionally kept this book short. I want you to quickly
get what you need and get on your way. As a bonus at the end,
I've given you thirty days of journal prompts. I recommend you
block off some time to commit to finishing this book and the
exercises. Then start on the thirty days of journaling. But before
we cover all of this, I have a couple of important notes for you.

First of all, please find a trusted, wise (and hopefully funny)
therapist. This will help more than you can imagine. BetterHelp.
com is a great resource if you don't want to ask your friends for a
referral. Many insurance plans offer some form of mental health
coverage; be sure to call your provider for specifics.

case no one has told you, it's okay if you need
depressants or anti-anxiety medication. Right now you're
rowning, my dear. But with a life raft like medication, you
can at least rest your legs for a little bit. We need you alive and
functioning. Your kids need you to be able to get out of bed
and laugh at their not-very-funny jokes. So please work with a
therapist and your doctor during this really difficult time.

I'll be sharing my personal story with you here in these
pages. It's very tender and I've tried hard to protect the father of
my children and his reputation. I wish I could share every detail
with you but unfortunately, my kids can read now. Instead, I'll
use discernment on what to share. But if you ever want the real,
real story, we can have coffee.

For my male, widowed, and child-free readers: Parts of this
book are absolutely for you. I don't have your experience, but I
have walked with friends through journeys like yours. I'll share
tactical pieces to rebuild your life here that I hope you find
helpful.

A note for my digital readers: You can absolutely use this
ebook with the exercises and prompts with any journal of your
choice. If you want the journaling pages in a PDF for printing,
you can find that here deidraromero.com/workbook.

I suggest you buy a package of colored pens from Amazon.
My favorites are Le Pens. Multi-colored pack is a must.

If no one has told you recently: You are going to be okay.
You will get through this. Your divorce will not define your life.
This is your chance to reawaken and create a new life from the
ashes.

Deep breath. Exhale. Let's go.

Chapter 1

10 THINGS YOU SHOULD KNOW ABOUT GRIEF BUT NO ONE EVER TAUGHT YOU

"Only grieving can heal grief; the passage of time will lessen the acuteness, but time alone, without the direct experience of grief, will not heal it." — Anne Lamott, *Small Victories*

In one of my first sessions post-separation with my therapist Sharon, I was talking about the losses piling up around me. Divorce doesn't just rob you of your marriage, it robs you of your identity, security, family, and future.

"This is grief," she said.

I think I'm a smart person. But until that point, I hadn't realized that losing my marriage (and my entire life basically) was sending me into grief. I didn't know anything about grief. I have lived a privileged life. I knew little about loss before my divorce. I hope these ten things I learned will create a perspective shift for you, too, about the recovery work that's in front of you.

1. GRIEF DOESN'T GO AWAY.

Shit. I know this sucks. The good news is it does hurt *less* often. The pain will persist. It will always be there, but it won't be as

1

intrusive as it is in your life now. Instead of the grief shrinking in your life, your life gets bigger and the grief remains.

Your life will expand around your grief, so it becomes part of your existence. This doesn't mean you will always feel sad or angry or confused. You won't.

2. YOU CAN'T MAKE GRIEF SMALLER BY NOT FEELING IT.

Not feeling your feelings around grief will not make them go away. Feelings are meant to be felt, acknowledged, seen, and witnessed. When we don't feel them, we just use energy trying to keep them at bay. One of my favorite teachers about mindfulness, feelings, and grief is Kris Carr. She just so happens to be my friend and former boss, too. In her book *I'm Not A Mourning Person*, Kris writes about how useless it is to try to stop our feelings. It's like holding a wave back. You will never be able to do it, even if you spend all your energy trying. Kris writes,

> *There's no real protection from painful feelings … the act of holding them back is equally painful and draining. It also takes an enormous amount of work—energy that's far better spent healing rather than resisting. Plus, as the Star Trek wisdom goes, "resistance is futile." One way or another, the waves of pain will eventually hit you. Managing those waves one at a time is far easier.*

3. THIS GRIEF AND THESE BIG SCARY FEELINGS WILL NOT KILL YOU.

I know this does not *feel* true. When I am in a grief spiral, I am convinced I will go to sleep and not wake up. Or worse yet, that my mental health is going to slip so far downhill, I won't be able to recover it. Feelings truly are like waves. They have a trough and a crest. It's true that dark feelings can get us in a funk for

2

days, but you can actually learn the skills to help you ride those scary waves, so you always land on a sturdy shore.

4. GRIEF WILL SHOW UP DURING YOUR HAPPIEST MOMENTS.

This doesn't even seem fair. And yet, it's true. Sometimes grief smacks me in the face when I'm roasting marshmallows with my kids in our backyard fire pit. We are all in good moods. The weather is perfect. The smoky smell of leaves burning is conjuring every perfect autumn memory from my childhood. And yet, the thought will creep in, *I wish I had a partner to share this with.*

This is normal. Joy illuminates the things we lost or what's still missing. I feel it every time something good happens in my life. Every Christmas. Every birthday. It just is. But the circle of my life has expanded to accommodate the grief.

5. GRIEF MEANS YOU ARE EXPERIENCING THE FULL SPECTRUM OF LIFE.

If you are only seeing part of the rainbow, you're not seeing a rainbow. Life is the same way. Suffering helps us embrace the beautiful, calm, happy, wonderful parts of our life. And it allows us to create space for the suffering of other people around us. If there is a purpose in suffering, it is to alleviate, eliminate, and witness the suffering of others.

6. GRIEF NEEDS A WITNESS.

I don't know why this is true or if it's even true for everyone, but it's been true for me. Suffering alone silently never helped me move through my grief. When I was overwhelmed by the grief, I would text a close friend, "I'm really hurting right now. I don't need you to do anything, but I want someone to know this, so I'm not suffering silently." And immediately I would feel the weight lessen.

3

Kris Carr said it beautifully in *I'm Not A Mourning Person*, "Pain needs to be witnessed, not polished." We all long to have someone stand in solidarity with us, even if we can't express or understand the pain. We need people around us to acknowledge it and say, *I see you. I see your pain.*

Even though we might find it difficult to reach out and ask for help, it's essential to our healing. In Brene Brown's book, *Atlas of the Heart,* she writes, "The more difficult it is for us to articulate our experiences of loss, longing, and feeling lost to the people around us, the more disconnected and alone we feel. Talking about grief is difficult in a world that wants us to 'get over it.'"

7. GRIEF ISN'T LINEAR.

My friend Katherine had a therapist once that explained that grief is like a spiral staircase. You're circling around and around and it feels like you've been here before but the perspective is different because you're further up the staircase. I promise your grief will transform. As you work your way up the staircase, the anger will feel different. The sadness will feel different. It will hurt less often.

8. GRIEF IS YOUR CALL TO REAWAKEN TO YOUR LIFE.

Grief is an invitation to live life on a deeper level. It's your call to reawaken to your desires and dreams. It is also an opportunity to realign your priorities. It is so tempting to numb out during the months of deep grief. That might look like excessive shopping, drinking, or binge-eating. Tune into those calls for "more." That's your soul asking you to do the work of healing. More food, more stuff, more alcohol won't heal you.

As Anne Lamott said in her TED Talk, "You can't buy, achieve or date serenity and peace of mind. This is the most horrible truth, and I so resent it. But it's an inside job." Happiness and

4

fulfillment are inside jobs. Getting "more" won't fix what's broken inside of you.

9. GRIEF WEARS A LOT OF MASKS.

Grief can look like chopping off your hair, selling your house, or dating that musician with the neck tattoos who lives in his van. Grief can look like bad choices or good choices, and it's okay if you can't tell the difference between the two. My friend Mary, a wise teacher and coach, told me that after my divorce I would go a little bit crazy. I thought, *Yeah, right. I have two children. How crazy can I get?* Goodness. I had no idea. Grief can lead to risky decisions at best and poor decisions at worst. In my grief, I definitely had seasons where I didn't care if I got abducted or my car got towed or if I drank too much. Apathy is a symptom of grief.

If right now in your grief you are making choices that aren't in alignment with your values, I get it. This is part of the process. The tectonic plates underneath you have shifted, and you are trying to find your footing.

Bad things happened to you. You are hurting. AND …

10. YOU ARE STILL RESPONSIBLE FOR ALL YOUR CHOICES.

Ugh. I know.

You are still in charge of you, no matter who hurt you or what he said or the text your former mother-in-law sent you. You will find your footing again. I'm confident this book and the work you are doing now will help.

Grief will make you a better friend, parent, and partner.

Before my divorce, I was terrified of all the big feelings. I didn't want to feel anything except okay and happy. This makes me sad now. I was robbing myself of a full life. Now that I've learned how to feel my feelings and I know they won't kill me, I can easily enter into the suffering of others. I can be present in difficult moments without needing to change the subject. I can hold emotional space for my children when they are upset. I can understand what great loss and great love feel like and know that I can bear it all.

Two of my closest friends ended their marriages prior to my divorce. They were in abusive, awful situations, and I fully supported their decisions to leave. But I definitely did not stand in the suffering with them. I worried about them. But I didn't check on them or show up or send them flowers just because. People did that for me, though. They entered into the suffering and held vigil on my behalf. They listened and cried and sent cards and traveled to take me out to dinner.

I've apologized to them both, but I still feel guilty. I just didn't know how to enter into their suffering. But now I do. Suffering builds bridges. It takes me to places I just could not access before.

Take some time to answer these questions to help you explore the ways grief is impacting your life right now. Don't forget, these questions are also in your Begin Again Workbook. You can download it now at deidraromero.com/workbook.

DIG DEEP

How is grief showing up in your life?

What does grief feel like in your body? Are you exhausted? Absent-minded?

Are you experiencing a desire to numb out? How do you deal when those feelings?

Which of these points about grief resonated the most with you?

Chapter 2

YOU ARE NOT ALONE

"We don't have to figure out how all of this works– 'Figure it out' is not a good slogan. It's enough to know it does." — Anne Lamott, *Help, Thanks, Wow*

If you are a person of faith or you have any seedling of belief in something bigger than yourself, I encourage you to lean heavily on it during this time. Some mornings I still wake up with a sense of, *This isn't the life I wanted*. And then I remember, *I am exactly where I'm supposed to be*. God has somehow cleared the path ahead of me and put the right people in my way. He's opened up the best opportunities, with some prayer and seeking. He has provided. He is faithful. His abundance is real. And he sees and knows my suffering in ways no one else does.

Maybe you don't have a faith of your own, or you struggle to believe in the goodness of a creator after so much loss and heartbreak. I encourage you to borrow my faith for a bit. Try it on for size, but leave the tags on. *Why am I insisting?*

My friends who don't have a sense of a loving God who is on their side have struggled the most in their divorce recoveries. They believe they are on the hook for manifesting their own healing. The best news I have for you is this: healing is our birthright given to us by our creator. We have a responsibility to do the work of recovery and make amends, just like an alcoholic in AA. But our healing is a co-creation with the divine.

I am okay in the world because of my relationship to the divine. Some days I have to tell myself, *I don't know what is ahead, but I know it's good.* If that's all the faith you can muster, that is plenty.

I am so guilty of forgetting that miracles are possible in my own journey. I get so caught up in what books I am reading, my self-care routines, and my therapy that I forget the spiritual aspects of my recovery. Belief in something bigger opens me up again to miracles, huge perspective shifts, and more than anything—a sense that I can relax. The pressure to heal and figure out my life isn't just on my shoulders. What great, good news.

Before my husband moved out of our family home, I'd known it was coming for two months. He'd already made the plans, put the deposit down on his new apartment, and hired an attorney. He moved upstairs into the guest room. Every day felt like Groundhog Day. I wasn't ready to give up on the marriage. I couldn't let go.

I won't go into details, but in the middle of an argument during that time, I had a moment of pure clarity. I knew in an instant the marriage was over and for both of our benefits it was absolutely necessary to end it. Certainty is a miracle. Clarity is a divine gift. I received both in a moment, and I was able to start making decisions from a place of strength and wisdom. Only God can do these kinds of things. These are the miracles I want for you, too.

I did nothing special or magical to manifest that miracle. I definitely didn't earn it. I had a tiny seedling of faith that God was still on my side. And it was plenty.

Chapter 3

THE AUTOPSY

"But where do we even start on the daily walk of restoration and awakening? We start where we are. We find God in our human lives, and that includes the suffering. I get thirsty people glasses of water, even if that thirsty person is just me." — Anne Lamott, *Help, Thanks, Wow*

Everyone I know who has gone through a divorce does this thing where they compulsively replay the entire relationship over and over again. I call it the autopsy. I would do this every single night in the early days of my separation. I would wake up at 1:00 a.m. and start the process again, looking for clues as to when the problem started. *Were there signs I missed? Were we doomed from the start? Did I marry the wrong person?*

Following the autopsy, I tried to assign blame. I wanted to know the truth. What did I do wrong? How can I prevent it from happening again? Was I an awful partner? At the time my husband moved out, I truly believed everything was my fault. I had ruined the marriage because I was a bad wife.

My friend Heather was the first person I divulged this to. She drove four hours to my house to stay the night. I shared with her my confession that it was, in fact, all my fault. I had been an awful wife. I had driven him away. She was stunned by my conclusion. She told me as delicately and as firmly as she could, "You're wrong. That's just not true." Her very tender challenge of my belief helped me consider the possibility that maybe it wasn't all my fault.

In one session with Sharon during this time, she encouraged me to stop trying to figure out who was responsible for what. "But I want to know what's mine to own and what's his, and it's just so fuzzy right now."

Yes, there will be a time and a place for that, but that's not where we should focus right now.

She was right. Eventually, it did fall into place. I started to see my own patterns and growth areas. I started to understand my full contribution to the dissolution of the marriage. One of my favorite relationship books is called *Conscious Loving* by husband-and-wife duo, Gay Hendricks, Ph.D. and Kathlyn Hendricks, Ph.D. They write about the principle of 100 percent responsibility—which can feel offensive at first glance, especially if you were a victim of emotional or physical abuse.

But stay with me here... there's something I think we need to take away from this principle to help us in our recovery. They write,

> *We ask that you begin with assuming that you are 100 percent the creator of everything that happens to you. You may have a dozen or more excellent arguments of why you are not responsible—your unhappy childhood, unfair coaches, dull parents, a bad neighborhood—but we want you to drop all those arguments for a while. As long as there is even one tiny part of you that thinks the world is doing it to you, the world is going to do it to you. When you know 100 percent that you create it you will start influencing the world around you in a much bigger and more positive way.*

One hundred percent responsibility is not the same as 100 percent blame. Wrongs were done to you. That is an unavoidable truth. You were damaged in this process. But I think we can hold these two truths together: **You were harmed AND you are responsible for your reality.**

I love the way Martha Beck puts it in her book *The Way of Integrity*, "While we may have been genuinely victimized, we never have to accept victim as an identity. We have the freedom to respond to every situation with creative thought or action."

When I was able to start to work from this crazy idea that I am 100 percent responsible for the reality I am creating, the work in front of me shifted. I stopped focusing on what Mark did or didn't do to me. I started taking ownership of my shit, and I realized that it's a new ball game now. I get to create the life I want for myself. But to get to that place, we have to make the mindset shift out of victimhood.

This is a real problem because victimhood benefits us in so many ways. Victimhood supports a story we tell about ourselves. We wouldn't tell it if it didn't benefit us. I know people who are several years past their divorces, some of them in new marriages, and they carried all their victimhood into their new marriages.

Victimhood for me meant that I could blame my divorce on my ex-husband. He's the one who filed, so he's the reason it all ended. But that's not entirely true. I was fully complicit in the relationship we created. I was fully responsible for the dynamics that existed in our home. The truth is, I was terribly codependent. I over-functioned in the marriage and allowed him to under-function. I was shut off from my feelings in a monumental way, which meant that real intimacy wasn't even an option for me.

Staying the victim allowed me to escape judgment for my divorce. It allowed me to be the pitied single mother (woe is me). It allowed me to stay stuck and hurt and gave me a pass on real life.

If you aren't sure if you're in victim mindset or not, there's one powerful question you can ask yourself: "Do I have a fantasy about being rescued from this situation?" This idea is also from Martha Beck. If you're stuck in victim mentality she suggests you "Say and do for yourself what you wish a rescuer would say and do for you." It is possible to be your own rescuer.

For those of you who had an unfaithful spouse: This is the ultimate betrayal. You truly were harmed in a deeply traumatic way. You were victimized. You didn't create the affair. Just as you are 100 percent responsible for your reality, so is your former spouse. The victimhood narrative is going to be a difficult one for you to get rid of. Staying in the victim mindset will only continue to cause you harm. Moving out of it will take decisive action and retraining your thoughts.

Every time you find yourself replaying all the wrongs that were done to you, I want you to capture those thoughts and replace them with a mantra. Mine went like this: "I am 100 percent responsible for the reality I'm creating right now."

Get this tattooed on your arm if you must. Other good mantras I've used:

I'm responsible for myself. He's responsible for himself. I can only control the way I behave.

Even though I was harmed, I am choosing not to be a victim.

Victim mindset doesn't serve me or the person I want to become.

I used to close my eyes and visualize myself standing in a circle, and a few yards away, I would picture my ex in his own circle. And I would say, sometimes out loud, "Everything in this circle belongs to me. And everything in your circle belongs to you." This exercise helped me create ownership over my own circle while separating myself so I could sever those codependent bonds I'd built.

In the questions below, we'll first uncover the ways victimhood is benefiting you. Then we'll work together to establish 100 percent responsibility for our realities. Set a timer for fifteen minutes and write as much as you can. Retraining your mind out of a victim mentality isn't one-and-done. You'll need to revisit these questions again and again, especially when you feel stuck in your pity party.

Let me be honest with you. Four years later, I am still doing this work. Just recently I was talking about all the wrongs done to me in my divorce. And then I was flooded with a wave of conviction. That was an inComplete Story and didn't acknowledge my responsibility or the gifts I was given through recovery. It's okay if this takes you a lifetime to learn. The questions below are a good start.

DIG DEEP

These are all the ways I feel I've been harmed by other people through my divorce and separation.

List ways your victimhood benefits you. By staying a victim, I am able to:

What apologies are you hoping for? What are the magic words you wish your former partner would say to you?

In your best revenge fantasy, what happens to your former partner? What happens to you?

Who are you blaming for your current reality?

What's the story you tell yourself and close friends about what happened to you?

Now rewrite the same story and take ownership of your actions. Don't write anything about what anyone else did to you.

How is your victimhood holding you back from healing?

How have your closest people pitied you or praised you in this season? How are they contributing to your victim mentality?

When you look back at this season of your life, what do you want to be able to say about the way you felt, thought, and behaved?

Chapter 4

REFRAMING

"It really is easier to experience spiritual connection when your life is in the process of coming apart. When things break up and fences fall over, desperation and powerlessness sink in, which turns out to be good: humility and sweetness often arrive in your garden not long after." — Anne Lamott, *Grace (Eventually)*

Reframing is one of the most powerful tools at your disposal. And the best news is, it's free. Just like you're watching your mindset when it comes to a victim mentality, I want you to be on the hunt for opportunities to reframe your situations.

Some people think reframing is just finding the silver lining or living in denial. It's actually neither. Reframing is finding a new perspective on the same situation. It doesn't negate the bad or disregard the truth. Reframing is zooming out to see a fuller picture or getting a new pair of glasses. You'll be able to see the individual leaves on the trees.

My friend Marissa once paid thousands of dollars to have a raccoon removed from her house and then paid a few thousand more to repair all the damage he'd done. Instead of getting upset about the situation (which she had no control over) she kept saying, "I'm so glad I own a house that a racoon *could* make a nest in." That is reframing at its finest. It is zooming out and choosing to view the situation with a better lens.

When my husband filed for divorce abruptly, I was devastated. I thought my life was over. After he moved out, I started to slowly build a new life. And as crazy as it sounds, amazing things started to happen. I was becoming the person I most wanted to be. I was able to have experiences I had only dreamed about. I started hiking. I bought a new home and designed it exactly how I wanted. I learned how to bake bread (okay, so did everyone else during the pandemic). I created a life I loved inside and out. I learned to love myself. None of that would have been possible if I had stayed married.

The big reframe that changed everything was this: My divorce is actually an invitation to reset my life. This was a gift, even though it didn't feel like it at the time.

What if the thing you think is going to destroy you actually rebirths you?

I have found this to be true for my life over and over. In Christian spiritual practices there's a recurring theme of death and resurrection. We see this in the life of Jesus, but also in the symbolism of salvation, communion, and baptism. The old must pass away so the new can come. You can't have spring without winter. You don't get fruit without the death of the seed.

We don't get rebirth if we don't let things die. If you can start to shift your perspective just one degree, your world will start to open. If you invite opportunities and miracles to show up on your behalf, they will.

My friend Anna called me about eighteen months ago when her husband suddenly filed for divorce. Her story was so familiar it was scary. She was devastated. I told her, "I know it doesn't feel like it now, but he's doing you a favor. We will be having a totally different conversation in a year."

Over the next year, she reclaimed her life. She got into therapy. Started doing things she loved that her ex-husband thought were stupid. She bought herself a home she loves. She was able to shift into *reset-my-life* mode instead of *I'll-*

never-recover-from-this mode. That reframing from disaster to opportunity was the magic switch that flipped.

A year later she texted me, "I will officially be divorced in seven days. My life is freaking thriving!"

Productivity guru and leadership coach Michael Hyatt asks his clients this question when they are facing huge challenges (and I think it is really powerful!), *What is the gift in this?*

That one question reframes everything into an opportunity.

At the end of 2019, I was developing my 2020 goals, which is laughable now because none of us knew what was coming in just a few months. I realized all my goals were financial or professional. I had no personal development or avocational goals because I didn't really have a life. For the seven years prior, I had been focused on keeping my marriage together and my kids afloat. *Who me? I'm just the one who keeps everyone else happy.* My only hobbies were occasional yoga and reading.

So, I decided 2020 would be my year of hobbies. I set a goal to try one hobby every month. Watercolor painting, pickling, bread-baking, kayaking, candle-making, hiking, just to name a few. And some of those hobbies actually stuck! I was able to open a new season of my life. I bought a cute red kayak and learned how to load it on top of my car all by myself. I even use ratchet straps, holy cow! I can't imagine what my life would be like without hiking. It's been such a gift in my life over the last few years.

Co-parenting and sharing my kids half the time has actually given me space to rest and have a life. That is a total reframe from my original feelings about co-parenting. I was devastated at the idea of having my children half the time. But because of the gift of time it gives me, I've been able to develop deeper friendships that I would have never had time to foster in my old life. I've been able to achieve more professionally and financially than I ever ever *ever* thought possible.

On a much deeper level, I love myself in a way I didn't think I could. This is probably the biggest gift of all. I have struggled with deep self-hatred since I was a teenager. It's something few people know about me. Sure, I like myself and I have good qualities, but love? Nope. That felt out of reach for me. It's really impossible to love and show up for a partner when you are not okay with yourself. Arguments with Mark would lead me into really destructive thoughts of self-harm. I couldn't handle our confrontations without becoming incredibly defensive and shameful.

One of the gifts of my divorce has been learning self-compassion. I don't beat myself up anymore when I make mistakes. If I feel shameful about something, I tell my friends every embarrassing detail because Brene Brown is right, "Shame unravels our connection to others." When I unpack my shame inside safe relationships, it loses its control over me, and I get to practice self-compassion. I am gracious to myself for my shortcomings. I trust myself in a rooted way that I never thought was possible. I will always bet on myself because I am always going to be here.

This life I have now is a gift, and I'm so incredibly grateful for the suffering and struggle that led me here.

I think it's possible for you to feel that way, too.

In my experience, reframing is only possible if you can stay out of blaming and complaining mode. When you drift into blaming and complaining, catch yourself in the moment and label it as blaming or complaining. Then, actively reframe that with a mantra. Or look at your arm tattoo.

Here's a real-life example where I caught myself recently. I had an overwhelming surge of anger at my ex when I was navigating some hard choices about a job transition. My thoughts went like this, *I can't believe he put me in this situation and forced me to be a single mother. I shouldn't be making all these decisions alone.* Can you see the blaming and complaining? Double whammy.

Now here's the reframe, *I am so thankful that I have wisdom and discernment to help me make these really hard decisions. I know, even if I was still married, these decisions would have been on my shoulders. I'm grateful I have people who I trust in my life to help so I'm not doing it all alone. These decisions are big opportunities I would have never sought out if I was still married.*

Hint: A lot of times, reframing looks like gratitude.

The questions below are going to help you start to reframe your divorce from a death to a rebirth. Take your time. You might need to do this work daily until it starts to become automatic.

DIG DEEP

What are the gifts or new opportunities you have right now because of your situation?

What's one thing available to you that you can take advantage of in this season?

List five new things you want to try (hobbies, restaurants, activities). Can you commit to one of these this month?

What do you want to be true in three months? How do you want to feel? What do you want to have accomplished?

What's one way you can show yourself compassion in this season?

What's one way you are holding onto blame right now?

Chapter 5

RESOURCE YOURSELF

"Most good, honest prayers remind me that I am not in charge, that I cannot fix anything, and that I open myself to being helped by something." — Anne Lamott, *Help, Thanks, Wow*

Asking for help is really, really hard. Especially if you are always the one helping and nurturing everyone else. As an experiment, try putting yourself into what I call an Automatic Yes mindset. This is so very hard and you're going to hate it at first. But here's how it goes.

Anytime someone asks if they can help you, you have to say yes. Without thinking. No matter what. You may not know how they can help you, but it's crucial that you say "Yes, I don't know what I need right now, but can I let you know?"

Why is this so important?

You need to open yourself up to community and connection. Do you remember your postpartum season? How fragile and tender your body was? How frayed you felt around the edges? Don't you wish you would have asked for more help as a young mother who literally just gave birth? I know I do. I look back at that season and think about how stoic (and stupid) I was. I didn't give myself any space for help and love. I thought I had to figure it all out on my own.

Denying help is the exact opposite of how we build connection with others. *Remember: Connection is essential to your healing journey.* Our suffering needs a witness. Our connection to others saves us from the clutches of shame. If you are going to make it as a single mom, you have to start saying yes and letting people in. There's no room for pride here. Your kids don't need a proud mother. They need a mother who isn't frantic and maxed out.

I want you to think about the different areas of your life that really matter to you. For me it looks like this:

Parenting
Work
Finances
Friends
Family (other than my kids)
Dating/Relationships
Hobbies
Home
Faith

You may have important hobbies or commitments that belong on this list. Every area of your life that you give energy to belongs on this list.

After I had my list, I started to build out a plan for each area, starting with this: Who do I know who can help me in this area?

For me, post separation, the financial piece was crucial. I had a colleague and a neighbor who worked in finance. I talked to each of them about what I should do with my house and how I should be handling my money. They offered me free advice and encouraged me more than they know! Three years later, when I was able, I hired a financial advisor to give me a more detailed plan.

There are people all around you with expertise and experience in the area where you need the most encouragement or confidence. One area for me was professional. I didn't have a professional mentor. This is actually something I'd been seeking for *years*. It felt like a big gap in my life. And then God sent me Lisa.

She was a client of mine who reached out shortly after my divorce. She was also divorced and had been a single mom for years. She came into my life with compassion, advice, and humor, and lit a path for me. I could see (for the first time) how my life *could* go. Talk about reframing. She was happy and successful and had even built a beautiful, blended family with her new husband and their five grown children. What an unbelievable gift she's been in my life.

Once you have your list, start thinking about who can help and encourage you in those areas. If it's a big blank, you need to ask. Don't panic. People you love actually want to help you.

If you are a person of faith, add this to your list of big asks from God.

It's essential that we build a little team around you, so you feel supported and cared for. Feeling alone in your single mother journey is brutal. My team looks like this. Please note: some of these people are paid consultants, therapists, and coaches I've found along the way to help me. Some are just old-fashioned friends and mentors.

Parenting/Co-parenting - Lisa, Maya, Liz, Georgi, Sharon

Work - Lisa, Blake, Cory, Suzie

Finances - Whitney, John

Friends - Liz, Maya, Cara, Heather, Betsy, Marissa, Katherine, Sarah, Nathan

Family (other than my kids) - Lisa, Sharon

Dating/Relationships - Angela, Marissa, Katherine

Hobbies - Katherine and Marissa, my book club

Home - Nathan, Contractor Brian, my dad

Faith - Church community, my mom

Now it is your turn. Think about all the big areas of your life and who can support you in those areas. Then I want you to make a list of questions or challenges you're facing in each area and where you still need support. Who could you possibly ask for help? Or is this an area where you need someone to come alongside you? Consider hiring someone if that's feasible. A good financial planner isn't as expensive as you'd think. I'm happy to share my list of resources of coaches and consultants with you if you need them!

DIG DEEP

Do you have an Automatic Yes mindset? If not, what's kept you from saying yes to offers of help?

Map out your life areas and a few challenges you have under each one. Write down two or three of your friends and family who could help you in that area.

Chapter 6

DEALING WITH RESENTMENT AND BITTERNESS

"Mercy means that we soften ever so slightly, so that we don't have to condemn others for being total shits, although they may be that." — Anne Lamott, *Hallelujah Anyway*

A lot of people equate forgiveness with healing. For me, forgiveness is a loaded word, and honestly, I don't know if I'm there yet. I battle daily with the temptation to fall into bitterness and resentment over my failed marriage. I am healed and I am healing. Both are true, and I know these truths because I do the daily battle.

Overcoming bitterness might be some of the hardest work you do in your lifetime.

But it is the work that will make or break your recovery. If you can just loosen your death grip on revenge ever so slightly, you will start to exhale deeper. It begins with wishing your ex-partner well. It took me years before I could think and say this with conviction: I hope he's happy.

Holding a grudge is like handcuffing yourself to your ex and trying to swim. You might stay afloat, but you won't thrive like that.

If you want a thriving, vibrant life, you have to let go of the resentment and the idea of cosmic revenge. I wish I had a four-step process for this, or some easy journal exercises. I don't.

My pastor once said, "You are allowed to walk the long road of what it takes to forgive someone who has hurt you." Forgiveness probably won't happen overnight. When it does, it's nothing short of miraculous. However, most often, it's a prolonged journey.

If you, little by little, every single day, choose to open yourself up to the possibility that revenge isn't going to make you happier, you'll start the process of letting go of your resentment. I believe this will lead you further down that road of forgiveness.

You might find yourself in a position where your ex is actively hurting you and your children. It is hard to move out of resentment and bitterness when your pain is constantly reinforced. Co-parenting is probably the only situation where you are forced to continue a relationship with a person who has perpetually hurt you and your kids. If this is your situation and you feel hopeless and confused about how to navigate it, please stop and seek help from a licensed professional with a specialty in abuse or co-parenting. You will continue to bang your head against this wall trying to make amends and heal while still stuck in the cycle of abuse—like brushing your teeth while eating Oreos. Please get help.

If that's not the case for you and your ex is just a mean, old-fashioned, difficult asshole who you don't like… keep reading. For years in my divorce recovery, I held on to the life raft that I was the "better parent." I wanted to believe that my ex husband's sins would find him out and all of the pain he caused me would result in my kids resenting him, too. *But guess what?* Hoping he fails miserably as a parent only makes me the worse parent. What I truly want now is for my kids to have a close-knit, safe relationship with their father. I want my kids to think back to their childhood and realize that they had two attentive, kind, amazing parents. That is the best outcome for all of us.

When we get stuck on what is owed to us as penance for our suffering, we are missing the point. Healing is what is owed to us. That is the big revenge at the end—that we and the people we love come out whole again. That is what it looks like when grace and mercy have the final say.

Rumi has this amazing quote I love, "Out beyond ideas of wrongdoing and rightdoing, there is a field. I'll meet you there." If you can co-parent from this posture, you are headed in the right direction.

As far as forgiveness goes, I'm still walking that long road four years later. Stay tuned …

DIG DEEP

How are your bitterness and resentment holding you back?

Think about your ex-partner healing and recovering, growing from their mistakes and living a prosperous, fulfilling life. How does that make you feel?

Revisit your revenge fantasy from Chapter 3. How will you feel if that doesn't happen, and the above scenario plays out?

Put yourself five years into the future. What is the best possible scenario for you, your ex, and your children?

Chapter 7

COMMUNICATING WITH YOUR EX

"We get to keep starting over. Lives change, sometimes quickly, but usually slowly." — Anne Lamott, *Help, Thanks, Wow*

In my early days as a mother of one, I had the most brilliant, loving group of moms around me. We all lived near each other and walked to the park almost every day with our kids. We met when our first babies were little. My son was a year old. These memories are so sweet. We built a little family of sorts and survived early motherhood and many subsequent pregnancies because of this group. It felt almost tribal.

One night at dinner with all of us and our spouses (this was rare), we started talking about how difficult this whole parenting thing is. Our friends Lauren and Spencer had just had their second baby a few months before. Lord, were they tired.

"How do you do it?" I asked. I couldn't understand the logistics of caring for two children all the time. My brain couldn't comprehend adding a baby to our family.

Spencer's response, "You just find another gear."

Lightbulb. I have applied this little lesson to every transition of my life. We just find another gear. Right now you probably can't imagine life as a single or co-parenting mother. Trust me when I say, you'll find another gear.

I especially apply this principle when talking about my relationship with my ex. How do you go from eleven years of marriage, making every decision together, intertwining your lives, to living totally separate?

You find another gear.

There is another mode to your relationship with your ex and, with a little bit of trial and error, you'll find it.

This is key for you to know: Every divorced couple has their own post-divorce relationship mode. My friend Sarah regularly invites her ex over for dinner. My friend Liz avoids talking to hers at all costs.

I decided early in my divorce that I needed to draw a big circle of protection around myself from my ex. I was incredibly codependent, fixated on his opinions of me. I had such a strong desire to make him happy at any cost. The only way I was going to heal that was to break away emotionally and put up some strong boundaries. Now we only talk about things that concern the children.

Some people want to be friends with their ex. They don't hate them, and they don't mind being around them. I don't have this aspiration. I want things to be peaceful and amicable. That feels like abundance to me.

My friend Russ describes his relationship with his ex like this: "She's like a coworker that I tolerate." I love this.

You might have a really hurtful or destructive communication pattern with your ex. Early in our separation this was the case for me, too. I had to communicate a couple of times that I was no longer interested in *talking about the marriage,* and I only wanted to focus on the kids. I drew a boundary that I wouldn't participate in those conversations any more. Thankfully he respected it and we were able to find a new gear of co-parenting.

Do whatever you need to do to protect yourself in your co-parenting relationship. I want to encourage you, (if it is possible) let your kids see you chatting and being friendly. I don't care if it's fake. You can submit yourself for an Oscar after the performance. Smile, be courteous, show your kids that they don't have to worry about you and dad. They need this foundation, especially if they witnessed a lot of turmoil during the divorce.

Communication with your ex is really, really hard. It's crucial that you show up in a way that feels good to you. Stay out of blame. Don't get petty. I always think of that Michelle Obama quote, "When they go low, we go high." When he goes low and starts to blame or criticize, you go high. How exactly do you do that?

If you can master this one principle, you'll win every time. This big idea of assuming positive intent comes from the book *The Loyalist Team*. It's a work principle, but it applies to every relationship I've ever had.

When you assume positive intent, you are assuming that your co-parent didn't do what he did maliciously. Here's how that might look.

When my daughter comes to my house after a long weekend and I find her lunchbox is growing hair, I could assume,

Oh, of course he did this on purpose. Geeze, what a jerk. He could have at least thrown out the food.

BUT what if I assume, instead, that it was an accident and there was no malintent?

Then my attitude looks like this.

Oh! He forgot to empty her lunchbox. I know they had a busy weekend. I probably would've forgotten, too.

Do you see how this protects your sanity and keeps you from attacking and blaming? Now I still might send a follow up text like this, *Hey I saw her lunchbox was pretty moldy. I know y'all had a busy weekend. I'm sanitizing it now and she'll be good to go.*

Zero blame, but I'm still holding him accountable.

This relationship with your ex will sharpen and refine your relationship skills like nothing else on this planet. **If you can find a way to be kind, courteous, and assume positive intent, you win. Not just inside of this relationship but with your kids in the long term.**

If you are awful and hateful to your ex, it poisons you and your children. Research shows that the childhood trauma from divorce is mostly caused by the arguing and conflict between the parents. Father wounds are so painful and take years to heal. Many of my friends still struggle with their father wounds into their thirties. If you can prevent your children from having a father wound by showing up at the soccer game with a smile and a coffee in hand for your ex, do it. That's an easy price to pay in my opinion.

One big tip I have for you as you're navigating co-parenting: over-communicate everything. Don't assume they put it in their calendar. Assume you forgot and never mentioned it. Here's an example.

When my kids have important things at school I try to mention it a couple of times in text to their dad and I send a calendar invite over. *Why chance it?* He is also good at over-communicating and confirming things with me. I forget stuff all the time. I'm juggling a million things at once and I appreciate the over communication. I know he does, too. Once we got into this rhythm, it became much easier for us to co-parent together.

DIG DEEP

What do you want your relationship with your ex to look like?

What kind of relationship with your ex would benefit your children the most?

Looking ahead at milestones in the lives of your kids, what do you want to be true about how you carried yourself at their graduations and weddings?

How might your actions or words about their dad create a father wound for your kids?

What are some boundaries or commitments to yourself that you need to establish to help you co-parent better?

Chapter 8

TELL A COMPLETE STORY

"Pretending that things are nicely boxed up and put away robs us of great riches." — Anne Lamott, *Stitches*

A lot of divorce recovery resources that I've seen out in the wild encourage divorced women in this way, *Your ex will regret ever leaving you. He's a loser. You're off to bigger and better things.*

While it might be true that your ex is a total loser, I'd like for you to adopt a Both/And mindset. Both/And Mindset believes that two things can be true at the same time. This is truly expansive living when you've mastered this. A Both/And mindset would say, *Yes, I was hurt tremendously in my marriage and my ex didn't treat me well. He is a loser. AND I also hope he heals and gets to live a really good life.*

Remember this, "When they go low, we go high." Or as The Message translation of the Bible reads, "If you see your enemy hungry, go buy him lunch; if he's thirsty, bring him a drink. Your generosity will surprise him with goodness, and God will look after you." Some translations read "for you will heap burning coals on his head." I like to think the burning coals symbolize the person's own conscience burning. Here is the bottom line. We don't get ahead when we wish ill on the people who have harmed us. We get ahead by reaching deep into ourselves and finding grace and generosity.

If you want to be a woman who is resilient and not jaded, this, my friend, is the treatment.

It is crucial that you learn to tell what I call a Complete Story about your life. This is probably the hardest skill to master of the ones I've talked about in this book. Narrative is so important when it comes to our healing. The way I tell the story of my divorce and recovery is directly tied to my mindset. Here are two narratives. One is a lop-sided story of my divorce and the other is a more Complete Story.

Mark and I met, and we were doomed from the start. We are from two really different backgrounds and families of origin. We had everything you could ever want—amazing careers, a gorgeous home, two beautiful kids. One day he just decided he was done, and he filed for divorce really quickly. He blew up my life.

All of this is true. But it's not a Complete Story.

Mark and I met and fell in love immediately. He was everything I was hoping to find in a husband. We wanted the same things, and we had a really beautiful wedding. I felt cherished and loved by him. Over time, very slowly, things started to shift. Life got a lot harder and I shut down. I didn't show up as the spouse I wanted to be, and I no longer felt cherished and cared for. I felt abandoned. It was not the kind of marriage I wanted. We were stuck in a destructive loop. I was really shocked when he filed for divorce. It sent me into a tailspin, and I thought my life was over. But it was actually an invitation to hit reset on my life and heal in a lot of ways. I still don't fully understand why he left so quickly or what was going on with him, but I'll probably never know that.

These are two vastly different stories. The first one rewrites history because it makes me feel better—if the marriage was doomed from the start, I don't have to accept any responsibility. Bonus Tip: If you're ever dating a man and he says this about his former spouse, "We never should've gotten married," tune in because he may be shirking responsibility.

38

Dr. John Gottman is one of the leading researchers about long-lasting relationships and divorce. His lab is famously known as the "love lab," where he and his colleagues watch couples interacting in seemingly everyday conversations. Gottman has said that he can accurately predict if a couple will get divorced based on just a few things. It's pretty amazing. I highly recommend his book *Why Marriages Succeed & Fail.* I'm proof that it alone won't save your marriage (I read it in college!) but it is really interesting.

One of Gottman's principles is The Four Horsemen of the Apocalypse. Basically, these are the four signs that your marriage is disintegrating and heading for divorce. One of the signs is rewriting history. When couples do this, they start to change their origin story from, *We had the best wedding. It was so gorgeous,* to, *I can't believe he wore that hideous tux to our wedding when I told him I didn't like the vest. I should've known this was never going to work out.*

Rewriting your story is probably something you've already started to do without knowing it. This is actually a tactic you're using to help you heal. It's not bad. Let's get that cleared up. It's valuable because if you are able to reject the past, you can move forward easier. I caught myself doing this after a recent breakup. I made a mental list of all the reasons it wouldn't have worked out long-term. I did this to help me move forward and get over my disappointment and rejection.

After my marriage ended, my story was this, *I married the wrong guy. I chose wrong.* My best friend Betsy really burst this bubble for me, saying, "I was there. I saw you fall in love. It was real. You didn't choose wrong."

Learning to tell a Complete Story isn't lying or denying what happened to you or what your experience was. Telling a Complete Story recognizes the way you might be rewriting your history. If you feel yourself getting activated and defensive as you're reading this, please know your Complete Story might sound like this:

I was trapped in a cycle of abuse. I was so young when we met, and I was hurting and depressed and he gave me comfort and attention that I was seeking. I was completely in love with him and then he started to physically hurt me. I stayed for four long years because I truly believed he would change. He could be so kind and caring, and he was a wonderful father, but he hurt me deeply.

When you tell a Complete Story you look at the good, the bad, and the unknown. You acknowledge all the suffering and the joy you experienced. This one simple exercise does a few powerful things at the same time. It gets you out of the victim seat. It helps you take 100 percent responsibility. And it helps you "go high."

You'll know you're telling a Complete Story because every part of you will agree with it. You won't have that tiny voice that says, "but what about …"

Here's the truth …

You *can* hold it all. You can hold the good and the bad in both hands. That's why you have two. If you really want to grow into your bravest self, you must learn this skill. There is no alternative option. Learning to tell a Complete Story will heal you in more ways than you can imagine.

DIG DEEP

Write out a first draft of your story. What was it like to be in your shoes? How did you feel?

What did your ex do well in your relationship?

What did you do well in the relationship?

Review your answers above. Underline any statements where you were blaming and villainizing others.

Next, put stars next to any positive acknowledgments you made.

What's missing from your story above?

What big unknowns are still present for you in your story?

Chapter 9

CREATE YOUR PLAN

"Periods in the wilderness or desert are not lost time. You might find life, wildflowers, fossils, sources of water."
— Anne Lamott, *Stitches*

As an Enneagram 3, this is my favorite part. I love planning and making plans happen. Once you start to shift your mindset, you can start to think and dream about what's ahead. I remember a moment after my divorce when I was getting dressed for a date. I was so excited and feeling all the anticipation in that moment was such a relief. I thought, *Oh, this is what's on the other side of all of this grief. Moments like this!*

Goodness. What a pinprick of light that moment was. I don't know what is ahead of you, but I know if you're doing this very hard work of healing and recovery, it is good.

It is good.

It is good.

It is good.

There's a tattoo for your other arm. I say this all the time, "I don't know what's ahead, but it is good."

If making plans feels overwhelming or daunting to you, skip to the next chapter. You can come back here when it feels lighter. When we're thinking about setting goals or milestones,

I want you to think about how you want to *feel* first. If we can tap into how you want to feel, we can start to create milestones or little goals that will help you get that feeling.

When you are deep in recovery, working toward goals will keep you moving forward. We want momentum in your life. If we can create that by putting a carrot in front of your face, let's do it. *Work smarter, not harder.*

First, choose your time increment. You can make milestones for the next three months, six months, a year, or three years. How far ahead can you see? When does it feel overwhelming? That's where you should stop.

I started with a year. I wanted to feel like I had a plan. I wanted to feel like there was some calm from the chaos. I wanted to get out of survival mode and start feeling some relief from the grief. I wanted to feel joy. I also wanted to feel like I was getting on firm financial ground.

After you establish how you want to feel, think about what you want. This might be hard for you. Especially if you're a recovering codependent. (Heyo!!) Try to focus on what you want and need. Not what everyone else wants and needs.

I knew I wanted a few things. I wanted to figure out what to do with my kid-free time after their dad started taking them half the time. I wanted to grow my friendships. I wanted to start dating. I wanted to sell my car and buy a new one. I also wanted to find a new church to attend.

I divided these up into the life areas where they fit. Glance back at your life areas from Chapter 5. This is how it looked for me.

Parenting

Work

Finances - Sell my car. Buy a new one.

Friends - Grow friendships.

Family (other than my kids)

Dating and Partnership - Start dating.

Hobbies - Figure out how to fill up my time.

Home
Faith - Find a new church.

Don't try to fill up every area of life with a milestone or goal. You won't be able to do anything successfully if you do too much.

Next, tie your feelings back to your goals with this phrase, "So I can feel _____." Remember, we're focusing on getting you a feeling, not a thing or accomplishment. I think when we ground our goals in feelings, we can understand why they are valuable and how they serve us.

Finances - Sell my car. Buy a new one. So I can feel more in control of my finances.

Friends - Grow friendships. So I can feel closeness and connection.

Dating and Partnership – Start dating. So I can start to feel excited about my single life.

Hobbies – Figure out how to fill up my time. So I can feel like I'm not in survival mode and I actually have a life.

Faith - Find a new church. So I can feel supported in my spiritual life.

For your next steps, I want you to list two or three action steps you're going to take to help you achieve these. They can be tiny, tiny, itty bitty to start with. Then slap a due date on it. Watch what I did.

Finances - Sell my car. Buy a new one. So I can feel more in control of my finances.
1. Look online at Carmax.com to see what I think I want.
2. Call my bank to get pre-approved.
3. Go to Carmax and test drive cars.
    Deadline: Complete steps 1–3 in 3 months.

Friends - Grow friendships. So I can feel closeness and connection.
1. Reach out to Katherine about having dinner.
2. Start a book club?
3. Host a dinner party.

Deadline: Complete 1 and 3, maybe 2 in 6 months.

Are you starting to see how it looks? Some people have awful associations with goals, and they hate goal-setting. Think of these as milestones getting you to the life you want. It is essential that you craft a plan to help you keep moving forward. My boss Kris used to say, "Set your goals so low you can trip over them." That is what I want for you. Especially in the first three to six months post-divorce. If you feel like you're ready for more than just three and six month goals, I want to encourage you to start writing your life vision. These are simple statements about what you want to be true for you in every area of life in the long-term. It took me quite a while to be able to develop this. I'll share a snippet of my vision with you here:

I have a full and beautiful life. It is vibrant with dedicated and kind friends, interesting books, new adventures, good food, amazing travels, a comfortable home, and many hobbies. Life is fun.

My kids are healthy, thriving, and growing in wisdom every day. They are always challenging me to become a better version of myself. They get along and love each other well.

My partner is attentive, funny, and engaging. We share an intimacy that is deep and fulfilling but we maintain our separateness and a sacred independence. It is the magic combination that keeps us excited to connect and get to know each other every day.

I am financially independent and debt-free. I have a small vacation home that is our haven on the water. We build memories there that will last and ripple through generations.

I can work from anywhere but choose not to sometimes. My job is fulfilling and impactful. I adore my co-workers and I feel motivated to do the work in front of me.

Open up the notes app on your phone and let yourself dream. No one has to see this. It can be our little secret.

Chapter 10

CREATE A GLOSSARY

"We are invited to be part of creation, like planting shade trees for children whose parents were born last week." — Anne Lamott, *Hallelujah Anyway*

When I first heard the term Divorce Recovery, it was like a lightbulb went off. *OH! That's what I'm going through.* One important key for me to feeling purposeful in any season of life is naming that season and putting a container around it. I struggle when I don't feel like I have a deep purpose. But if I can name a season and give it meaning, it opens me up to accepting whatever that season has in store.

Before I close out this book I wanted to give you some of my favorite words I created to give my Divorce Recovery journey meaning, and help me understand what was happening in a better way. These are words I made up FYI, so don't throw them around and assume everyone knows them.

I encourage you to start naming your own experiences. If something stands out as unique, new, or different, try to label it so you can contain it and give it meaning.

Deep Divorce Recovery - This is the first year of your Divorce Recovery journey. It's the most tumultuous and heartbreaking. Painful doesn't even begin to describe it.

Maintenance Divorce Recovery - I think this is the phase I'm in now. I still bump up against the grief and pain every once in a while. Holidays are still hard. I don't know if this is how it will always be or if this also has an expiration date.

Grief Backpack - This term was a gamechanger for me. I like to think of my grief like it's a backpack. I'll always have it but some days it is lighter than others. When my grief feels extra painful and present, I comfort myself by noting that the grief backpack feels heavy right now but it won't always feel this heavy. The way we talk about our feelings and our experience matters! Using the grief backpack is one extra way you can share your experience with your friends and family.

Landmines - Birthdays and holidays are bombs in plain sight, but landmines are events or small things that you can't see that will explode in your hands. Examples: finding your wedding guest list on your hard drive, getting an email about airline tickets on sale to Italy (the trip you thought you'd take with your husband), or it could be as simple as coming home from a trip to a silent house. Landmines access a pocket of grief you didn't even know existed. And there isn't much you can do but acknowledge them and know there are more ahead. In the beginning you will find lots of landmines. But over time, even if you find one, it may or may not explode on you. Being able to label something as a landmine will help you process it.

One day I was looking for something deep in the bowels of my closet and found my divorce papers. It was a landmine that exploded in my hands. I didn't cry but it threw me off my axis for days. This is normal. You aren't doing anything wrong. You're a fully present, feeling, healing human. You're doing a great job.

Automatic Yes Mindset - This mindset is choosing in advance that you will say yes automatically to the manna from heaven that comes in the form of help from others. Don't even give yourself a moment to think about it. Just say yes.

Whiplash - My kids always return to me on Wednesdays. It's rough for everyone. I affectionately call it Whiplash Wednesday.

I lose my autonomy again and am in the throes of single motherhood. The house is instantly destroyed. I don't know how this happens. My kids are acclimating to a different house with a different set of rules and a different vibe. It's startling for everyone. Some Whiplash days are worse than others. I've found a few keys that make it easier for me and I want to share these here.

1. I always get myself out of the house before the kids come home from school on Wednesdays. Maybe it's the gym or a coffee run (I work from home), or lunch with a friend. Whatever it is, I create a little pocket of time for me to express some autonomy.

2. Caffeinate in the afternoon. I find Whiplash days kick my ass in the energy department. So, I make sure I have an afternoon coffee to get me through dinner, homework, clean up, and the big feelings that come out on Whiplash days.

3. No plans on Whiplash day. Once my daughter had soccer practice on Wednesdays and it was awful. Our entire day was jacked, bedtime was so late, and we were all in a funk the next day. I clear the decks on Wednesdays.

4. Make time for connection. I make sure I have at least twenty minutes to connect solo with each kid. For my daughter, we play right before it's time to get ready for bed. She gets to choose what we do. With my son, after my daughter is in bed, we make Sleepy Time tea and watch funny videos on Instagram.

5. Under NO circumstances are you to cook any kind of dinner. This is an ABSOLUTELY NOT. Don't even try it. Don't get high and mighty and think everyone is in a good mood, it'll be fine. Just trust me. It's never fine. No one will die if they eat turkey sandwiches and chips for dinner.

The Autopsy - This is the endless loop in your brain that replays every big and small event in your marriage searching for clues about what happened. It does stop eventually. I promise.

Complete Story - A Complete Story acknowledges the pain and reality of a situation and the joy and triumph. When you reflect on your marriage, don't leave out the good stuff or the bad stuff. It all counts.

Now let's work on creating your own glossary to help you navigate your healing.

DIG DEEP

What are some experiences you are having that are difficult for you right now?

Are there times of your day or week when you feel overwhelmed or struggling?

What names or titles can you give these difficult moments?

Chapter 11

25 THINGS THAT WILL HELP YOU ON THIS RECOVERY JOURNEY

ALL THE SMALL THINGS I WANT YOU TO KNOW

1. Start moving your body. Movement is the only way your body can complete the stress cycle. It is the cheapest and easiest way you can overcome anxiety and stress.

2. Start a journaling practice. Even if it's just a few sentences each day, it will make a big difference. Some research shows that journaling is just as effective as therapy. I've created thirty days of journaling prompts for you at the end of this book.

3. Create routines and rituals that make you happy. You have been drained dry of your life force. Your dopamine and joy are low. Find small things that give you a little boost. I love lighting a candle, getting a good book, pouring a glass of wine, and taking a long, pruney bath. This is a routine that

brings me so much comfort and joy. Do you know what makes you happy and brings you comfort? Tap into those things.

4. Stop talking shit about your ex. Trust me. No one wants to hear it. And you need to protect your heart.

5. Talk directly to your sadness. I do this a lot. It goes like this, "Hey sadness, I feel you. I really want to cry right now but I can't because I have to take this call for work. But I'm going to come back to you later tonight." Acknowledging your feelings in the moment and promising that you will

come back to them when it is convenient is a fantastic way to still feel your feelings but also be able to function.

6. If there's something strangely triggering about driving and you find yourself crying, that's okay. This happened to me, too. I always broke down in the car. My best friend Liz said this was true for her as well. This is a strange phenomenon. And if you Google, "why do I cry easily in the car," you'll fall into a Reddit hole. Good luck.

7. If dating post-divorce is too scary for you, that's okay. Move at your own speed. You'll meet someone when you're ready.

8. If you don't understand how you'll ever love again, that's okay, too. This healing process is going to expand your heart just like the Grinch, so you'll actually be able to love even deeper after this. Just you wait.

9. Close friendships are essential to your healing. We don't heal in isolation. We heal through connection and community.

10. Tell the whole truth as much as you can in every area of your life. A commitment to total honesty with yourself and others will keep you in alignment with your values.

11. Your kids are going to be okay.

12. You are going to be okay.

13. Your family will probably always hold on to resentment about your ex. You don't have to do this too. Letting go of the bitterness will open you up to fully heal.

14. Healing looks different for everyone. And we all move at our own pace. Some people are happily remarried two years after their divorce. There's no science here. Just imperfect people trying to do their best.

15. Get outside and walk or hike as much as you can. If you ever feel "off," your body is asking you for attention. Listen.

16. Your shame about your divorce will splinter your connection to others. The anecdote for shame according to Brene Brown is vulnerability. Open yourself up and tell the truth about

your experience, even if you feel naked and scared doing it. Do it anyway.

17. Learn how to pray and ask for help outside of yourself. Even if it feels decadent and indulgent. It's okay to want things.

18. Just because your kids come from a "broken home" doesn't mean they have to have trauma or behavioral issues.

19. If you're in a state of shock about this huge left turn your life just took, I promise that will wear off. It's going to take some time. You'll still wake up and have moments where you forget and then the grief slams into you again like a Mack truck. This will not always happen.

20. Some marriages and divorces are Traumatic with a capital T. If you think you might be experiencing symptoms of trauma, reach out to a therapist immediately. You can heal and recover from deep trauma, but your process is going to look a little different.

21. Slow down and find quiet. If you're co-parenting, it's so tempting to fill up every empty minute on your schedule.

This is okay at first, but eventually you need to slow down and sit in the quiet, lonely places. This hurts so much.

22. The loneliness might feel unbearable. A lot of times, it feels like a wolf at my door. My journey to accept and confront my loneliness has been a long one, but it's been worthwhile. Don't feel ashamed about this. You are finding a new way. If you can't stand to be alone right now, that's okay. But slowly, slowly, you'll need to invite the wolf inside and offer him a cup of tea. It turns out he isn't even hungry.

23. English economist and author Tom Harford said, "When you are forced to find a new way, you find a better way." This is backed up by mountains of research. You are finding new ways of doing everything right now. Trust that you are actually finding better ways.

24. Mindset is everything when it comes to healing. Remind yourself of the good. Keep a gratitude journal. Focus on your mindset and you'll be okay.

25. This book is not a comprehensive guide to your healing. It doesn't start and stop with these pages. Keep going. Even after you think you are "healed." Keep doing this recovery work. Hide nothing. Hold everything.

30 DAYS OF JOURNALING
USE YOUR WORDS TO HEAL

Of all the tools I had at my disposal during my divorce recovery there are three that propelled me toward healing: hiking, journaling, and therapy. Two of those are absolutely free! If you've never tried journaling before, I want to encourage you to try these thirty days as an experiment. If you hate it, you never have to do it again, but if you like it and it helps you feel better, then you've added another tool to your toolbox. *Also, did I mention it's free?*

Set aside ten minutes a day for these prompts. Pro tip: set a daily reminder on your phone until you've instilled the habit. If you skip a few days, totally fine. Just finish.

1. How do you envision your life post-divorce? Describe your

    ideal future.

2. What are the most challenging emotions you're experiencing right now? And how do they feel in your body?

3. What's one thing you really want to do that you couldn't do when you were married? What's stopping you now?

4. List three things that make you proud of your strength during this journey.

5. How has your relationship with your children changed since the divorce?

6. What self-care practices have you found most helpful in managing stress?

7. Describe a recent moment when you felt a sense of peace or happiness.

8. Write a letter to your children about your hopes for them when they look back at this season of life.

9. What new goals or dreams have emerged for you post-divorce?

10. Reflect on your coparenting dynamics. What's working, and what could improve?

12. What's one challenge you're facing right now that's taking up a lot of space in your brain?

13. What's one area post-divorce where you've experienced a win?

14. Describe a moment when you felt gratitude for your support system.

15. How has your sense of independence evolved since the divorce?

16. Write down five things you love about yourself.

17. Reflect on any personal growth or newfound resilience you've discovered.

18. If this happened last week or seven years ago, it doesn't matter. If you still need healing, this book is for you.

19. What hobbies or interests have you rekindled or discovered post-divorce?

20. How do you envision co-parenting successfully in the long term?

21. What lessons have you learned about love and relationships from your divorce?

22. Write about a memory or tradition you want to create with your children.

23. What still makes you mad about your divorce?

24. What kind of role model do you strive to be for your children?

25. Reflect on the support you'd like to receive and how you can ask for it.

26. Describe a moment when you felt proud of your progress in healing.

27. Write about a personal boundary you've established or plan to set.

28. How do you plan to prioritize self-care and self-love moving forward?

29. What's one dream you have as a single mother for your kids?

30. Write a letter to your ex-spouse, expressing your thoughts and feelings (do not send this!).

RECOMMENDED READING

Atlas of the Heart
Brene Brown

I'm Not A Mourning Person
Kris Carr

Stitches
Anne Lamott

Help, Thanks, Wow
Anne Lamott

Untamed
Glennon Doyle

ACKNOWLEDGMENTS

I want to thank my closest friends who were in the trenches with me: Liz, Heather, Betsy, Maya, Cara, Tiffany, Marissa, Katherine, Sarah, Lauren, MD, Cory, and Nathan. Thank you for the late night phone calls, constant texts, long dinners, trips away, glasses of wine, funny memes, plus your trust and adoration. Your partnership (and humor) gives me life.

Sharon, thank you for the good work you do. I don't even have the words. Our therapeutic relationship is a gift from God.

Lisa, thank you for being my mentor in every sense of the word. I prayed for someone like you for years. Your friendship and advice are invaluable.

Mom and Dad, thank you for being my biggest fans. Sorry for the colorful language.

AUTHOR BIO

Deidra Romero is a writer and mom of two. She's committed to helping single moms heal from divorce and lead amazing lives. You can follow her on Instagram @deidradaily or at her blog home DeidraRomero.com. When she isn't at her laptop, she's making dinner for friends, traveling somewhere with good food, or searching for local adventures with her kids in their hometown, Nashville.

Made in the USA
Monee, IL
14 September 2024